BOND
VILLAINS

BOND
VILLAINS
Alastair Dougall

CONTENTS

Dr. No ™

Investigating the disappearance of an MI6 agent in Jamaica, Bond confronts clandestine worldwide criminal organization SPECTRE and its Number 2 operative, the chilling Dr. No. With a web of assassins, a private army, and an island stronghold guarded by a legendary fire-breathing "dragon", Dr. No is determined that nothing and no one will interfere with SPECTRE's scheme to disrupt the US space programme and create a new world order.

I gave orders that Bond should be killed. Why is he still alive?

Dr. No

DR.NO

The prisoner, Bond, had been treated well, even invited to dinner. Dr. No's icy demeanour revealed little of his anger as Bond proceeded to mock his masterplan, his genius, even his mechanical hands, sacrificed on the altar of science. Bond would be no use to SPECTRE after all.

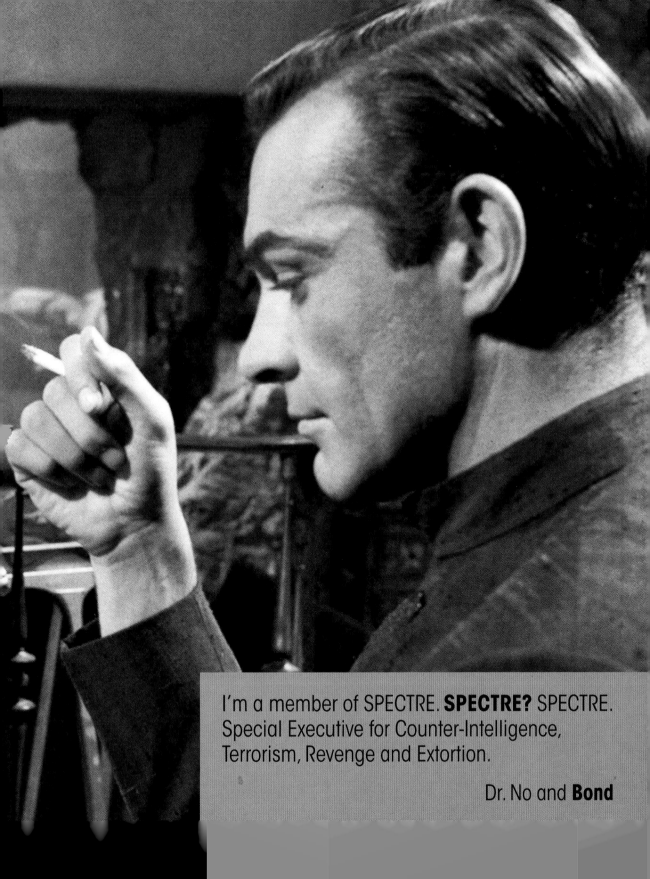

I'm a member of SPECTRE. **SPECTRE?** SPECTRE. Special Executive for Counter-Intelligence, Terrorism, Revenge and Extortion.

Dr. No and **Bond**

> Sit down.
> Why have you
> disobeyed my
> strictest rule and
> come in daylight?
>
> Dr. No

PROFESSOR
DENT

The distinguished-looking metallurgist controlled Dr. No's network of assassins. Panicked by Bond's enquiries, Dent sought his employer's advice. Dr. No provided him with a typically devious means of murder: a deadly tarantula.

Dent recoiled in horror as the disembodied voice of Dr. No ordered him to pick up the cage containing the spider.

FROM RUSSIA WITH L☭VE ™

Determined to take revenge for the death of Dr. No, SPECTRE hatches a fiendish scheme to discredit MI6, bring about Bond's "suicide" and acquire the Lektor, a secret Soviet decoding machine. The brains behind the plot are chess grand master Kronsteen and ruthless KGB defector Rosa Klebb. Muscle is supplied by SPECTRE enforcer Morzeny and assassin Donald "Red" Grant. All those involved know that failure will not be tolerated.

Must be a pretty sick collection of minds to dream up a plan like that.

Red wine
with fish.
That should
have told me
something.
**You may
know the
right wines,
but you're
the one on
your knees.**

Bond and **Red Grant**

RED GRANT

Bond's suspicions of "Captain Nash" had been well founded – he was SPECTRE assassin Red Grant. This merciless, methodical killer had been tracking Bond for some time. Bond's position was desperate, but perhaps he could tempt Grant with the gold sovereigns in his case – Q's special case with the trick lock…

ROSA KLEBB

Vicious and cruel, Colonel Rosa Klebb had secretly defected from the KGB to join SPECTRE. Recruiting a beautiful, innocent girl, Tatiana Romanova, to do SPECTRE's dirty work was just her style.

Klebb employed promises, threats and appeals to Tatiana's patriotic duty to trick her into participating in SPECTRE's plot.

Corporal, I have chosen you for an important assignment… And if I refuse? Then you will not leave this room alive.

Rosa Klebb and Tatiana Romanova

GOLDFINGER™

A crooked card game, the gilded corpse of a murdered girl, an ingot of Nazi gold and a switched golf ball mark crucial stages in Bond's pursuit of suspected gold smuggler Auric Goldfinger. Finally, Bond discovers the villain's masterplan. It is typically ambitious and ruthless: to detonate an atomic device inside Fort Knox and destroy the US's entire gold supply. In order to make himself ten times richer, Goldfinger cares nothing that thousands of innocent people and many of his own criminal associates will die.

My plan is foolproof, gentlemen. I call it Operation Grand Slam!

Goldfinger

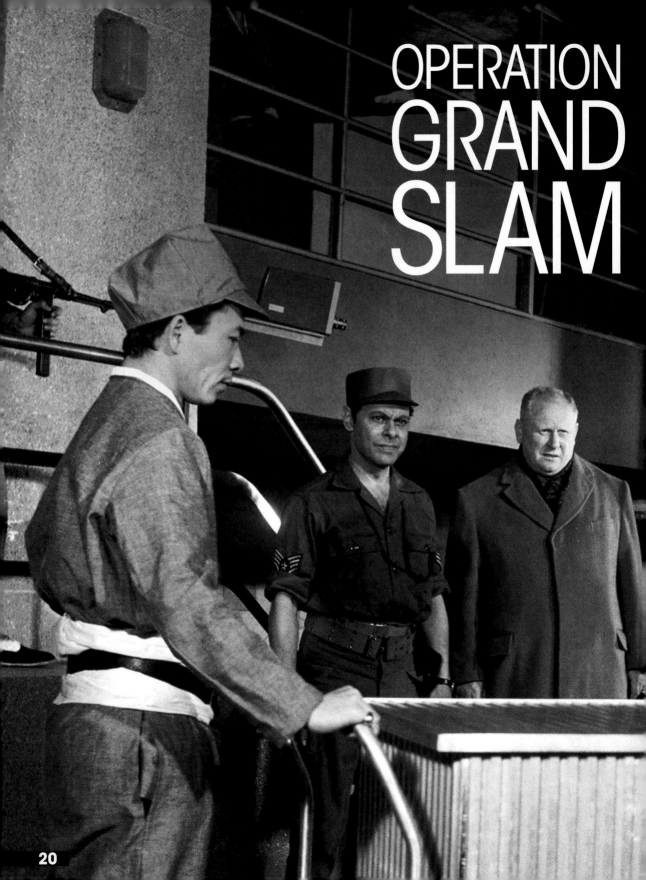

OPERATION GRAND SLAM

The operation had proceeded perfectly. Pussy Galore's Flying Circus had gassed the troops guarding Fort Knox. Goldfinger's guards had blasted through the perimeter fence and broken into Fort Knox with a laser. Finally, Goldfinger had arrived with the bomb that would irradiate the entire US gold reserve…
What could possibly go wrong?

ODDJOB

No villain ever had a more faithful servant than Oddjob. Despite being locked inside Fort Knox's gold vault by his master, Auric Goldfinger, along with James Bond and a ticking atomic bomb, Oddjob's loyalty never wavered. In minutes the bomb would explode and Goldfinger's plan would succeed. But first, Oddjob would have the pleasure of killing Bond.

Hugely strong, an expert in karate, Oddjob used no weapons, apart from the razor-sharp brim of his hat. He met his death reaching for it. Bond electrocuted him, using a power line broken during their epic struggle.

Where's your butler friend?
Oh, he blew a fuse.

Felix Leiter and **Bond**

THUNDERBALL ™

From his estate in the Bahamas, Emilio Largo spearheads SPECTRE's most ambitious project yet: hijacking two atomic bombs and holding the US and UK to ransom. Aiding Largo is Count Lippe – whom Bond soon gets the better of – and fiery femme fatale Fiona Volpe from SPECTRE's Execution Branch. When Largo and his divers transfer one of the bombs to his luxury yacht, Bond infiltrates the gang. Before long, SPECTRE's grandiose scheme is heading for the rocks.

SPECTRE is a dedicated fraternity whose strength lies in the absolute integrity of its members.

Ernst Stavro Blofeld

He is Bond and, as an enemy of SPECTRE, he should be killed.

Emilio Largo to Fiona Volpe

EMILIO LARGO

Bond was becoming a nuisance. He had ruffled Largo's feathers at the casino, flirted with Largo's mistress, Domino, and spied on Largo's yacht, the *Disco Volante*, vital for transporting SPECTRE's hijacked bombs. Bond had to be eliminated. Once he was out of the way, SPECTRE's extortion scheme would be plain sailing.

ROUGH TREATMENT

Bond was recuperating at Shrublands health clinic when he noticed the suspicious tong tattoo on SPECTRE agent Count Lippe's arm. Lippe tried to kill Bond on a traction machine, but Bond ensured that it was Lippe who got all steamed up.

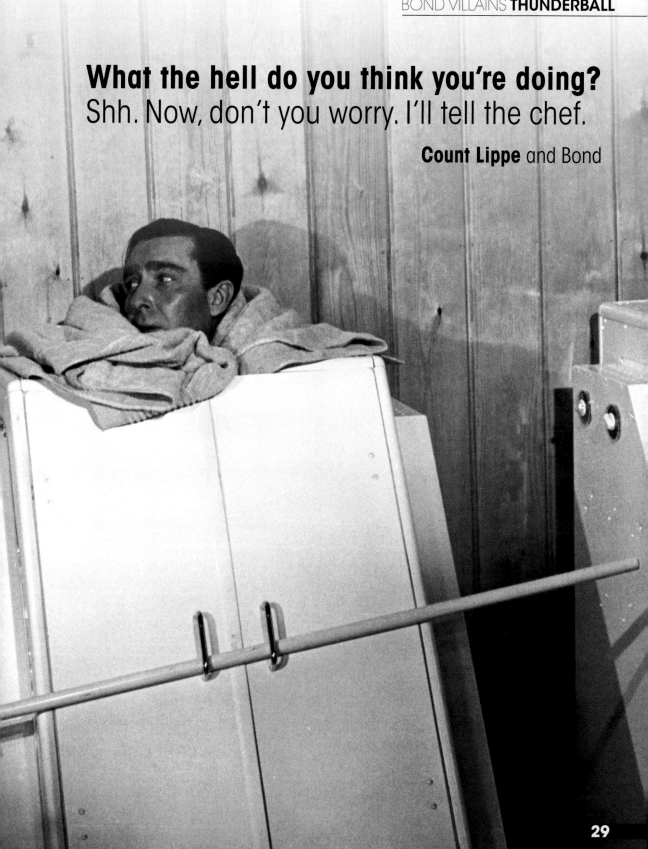

What the hell do you think you're doing?
Shh. Now, don't you worry. I'll tell the chef.

Count Lippe and Bond

YOU ONLY LIVE TWICE ™

Bond has fought and won three spectacular encounters with SPECTRE but never penetrated to the evil organization's heart, never met its merciless chief, Ernst Stavro Blofeld, face to face. That state of affairs is fated to change when M dispatches Bond to Japan to investigate the mysterious hijacking of a US spacecraft. The confrontation with SPECTRE's mastermind proves the most volcanic of Bond's career.

Allow me to introduce myself. I am Ernst Stavro Blofeld.

Blofeld to Bond

BLOFELD

The SPECTRE mastermind had believed he was impregnable. He had established a rocket base on a far-flung Japanese island, inside a dormant volcano. He had ringed the volcano crater with gun emplacements. Yet, despite all Blofeld's precautions, Bond had infiltrated this lair, meddling in SPECTRE's plan to foment war between West and East. But now, Blofeld was sure, Bond was in his power.

I shall look forward personally to exterminating you, Mr. Bond.

Ernst Stavro Blofeld

HELGA BRANDT

I'm awfully sorry to leave you, but I have to get off!

Helga Brandt
to Mr. Fisher, alias Bond

She was supposed to find out what "Mr. Fisher" knew and then kill him. SPECTRE assassin Helga Brandt decided to have a little fun with the handsome spy first. Afterwards, she pretended to go along with his plan to cash in on stolen secrets. A crashing aeroplane would make a fitting coffin for Mr. Fisher.

Helga Brandt did not have to use much persuasion to make Mr. Fisher own up to being an industrial spy.

ON HER MAJESTY'S SECRET SERVICE™

Ernst Stavro Blofeld had wearied of crime. He yearned for the respect he believed his genius deserved and the title of the Count de Bleuchamp. However, there was only one way his past misdeeds would be overlooked: he would have to blackmail the world. Blofeld decided to create a virus, Virus Omega, that could destroy crops and livestock, threatening economic meltdown.

It'll take more than cutting off your earlobes, Blofeld, to turn you into a Count.
I may yet surprise you… I know all about your mission…

Bond and Ernst Stavro Blofeld

BID FOR a TITLE

Blofeld was displeased. Sir Hilary Bray of the Royal College of Arms was a stickler for accuracy, unwilling to accept Blofeld's claim to be the Count de Bleuchamp without concrete proofs. Well, he should have them. Blofeld did not suspect, at the time, that he was trying to convince James Bond.

IRMA BUNT

Fanatically loyal to Blofeld, Fräulein Bunt had personally supervised the "Angels of Death", the beautiful, brainwashed patients at Blofeld's allergy clinic. Soon they would be free to unleash Virus Omega on the world. James Bond must not be allowed to interfere.

Irma Bunt looked on as the "Angels of Death" received Blofeld's final orders while under hypnosis.

Fancy meeting *you* here, Fräulein!

Bond to Irma Bunt

Diamonds Are Forever™
Forever
Forever

On the run from MI6 and Bond, Blofeld creates a new face and doubles of himself. He is only just in time. Bond drowns a double in mistake for Blofeld, leaving the master criminal free to embark on his latest outrageous scheme. Blofeld creates a satellite superweapon using a hoard of smuggled diamonds and technology stolen from kidnapped industrialist Willard Whyte.

I do so enjoy our little visits, Mr. Bond.
However potentially painful they may be.

Ernst Stavro Blofeld

Blofeld – or rather one of his doubles – seized a surgical knife and attacked Bond.

EVIL'S
NEW FACE

Bond was closing in – Blofeld could sense it. The operation to create doubles of his new physiognomy must be completed tonight. As if on cue, Bond arrived, seeking revenge for the murder of Tracy, his bride. Blofeld's plan to fake his own death and disappear swung into action.

WINT & KIDD

Blofeld was eager to cover his tracks by eliminating the key players in his diamond-smuggling pipeline. He let loose Wint and Kidd, his subtlest, deadliest killers. The pair's first victim was a dentist at a South African diamond mine.

The scorpion.
One of nature's finest killers, Mr. Wint.
One is never too old to learn from a master, Mr. Kidd.

Mr. Wint and Mr. Kidd

LIVE AND LET DIE™

Dr. Kananga exploits his position as president of the Caribbean island of San Monique to grow a vast opium crop in order to flood the US with heroin. The drug will be distributed through a restaurant chain run by Kananga's gangster alter ego, Mr. Big, with muscle provided by the ever-grinning Tee Hee. The plan seems foolproof, but Kananga has a weakness: he relies on the soothsaying powers of the beautiful, virginal Solitaire.

Mr. Bond. It's good to see you again.

Tee Hee

DOCTOR
KANANGA

**The question still stands, Mr. Bond…
Did you touch her?**

It's not the sort of question a
gentleman answers.

Dr. Kananga and Bond

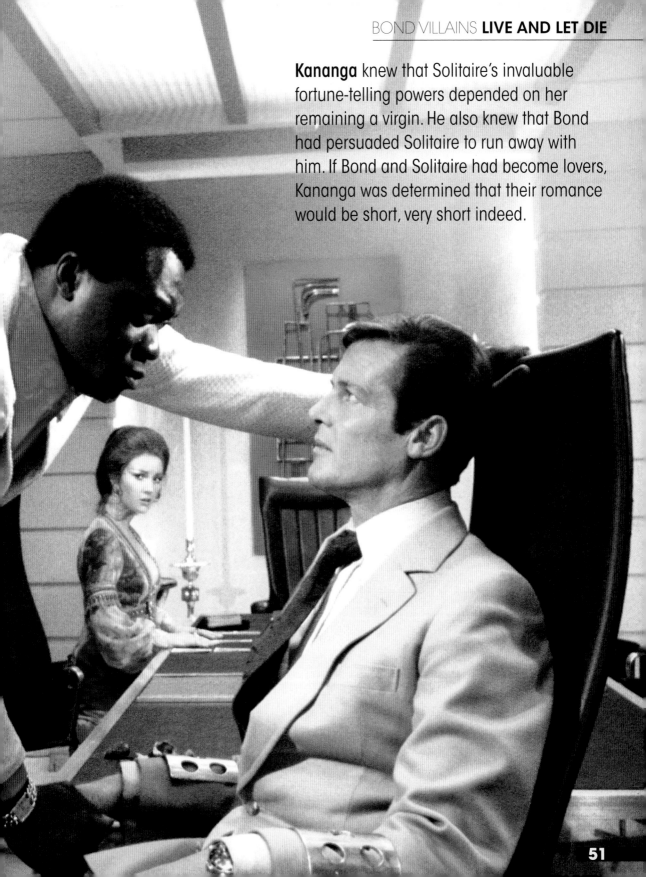

Kananga knew that Solitaire's invaluable fortune-telling powers depended on her remaining a virgin. He also knew that Bond had persuaded Solitaire to run away with him. If Bond and Solitaire had become lovers, Kananga was determined that their romance would be short, very short indeed.

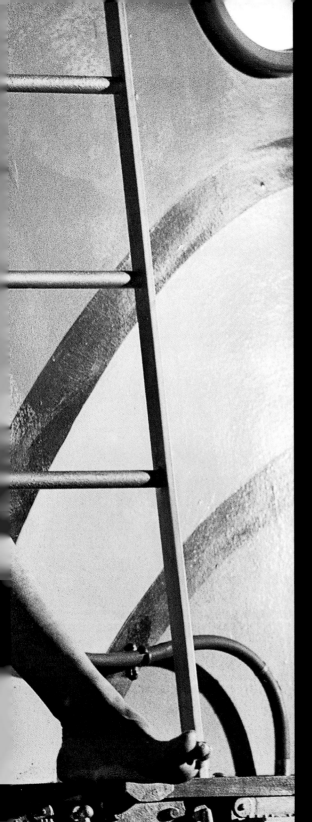

BARON SAMEDI

The Voodoo god of cemeteries, Baron Samedi
The Man Who Cannot Die, struck fear into the
people of San Monique. The country's presiden
Dr. Kananga, saw the advantages of this and
employed a man who claimed to be the
spooky Baron. Perhaps his boast was true…

Baron Samedi, or the man posing
as him, frequented the cemetery near
Dr. Kananga's headquarters. His flute
doubled as a communicating device.

THE MAN WITH THE GOLDEN GUN™

Scaramanga is the world's deadliest assassin, a killer who only needs a single gold-plated bullet. But being a gun for hire, however feared, has its limitations. Scaramanga now wants to call the shots himself. The death of his current employer, Bangkok industrialist Hai Fat, and the possession of the Solex Agitator, a revolutionary solar energy device, will enable him to taste real power. He can then pit his assassin's skills against the only man alive he considers a worthy adversary: James Bond.

What do you know about a man named Scaramanga, Double-O-Seven?

Scaramanga? Oh yes, the Man With the Golden Gun… Current price one million dollars a hit. No photograph on file, but he does have one distinguishing feature, however: a superfluous papilla.

A what?

A mammary gland. A third nipple, sir.

M and Bond

SCARAMANGA

Solar energy expert Gibson was planning to defect back to the British with the precious Solex Agitator. Scaramanga was dispatched to make sure that didn't happen.
The Man With the Golden Gun took up his position outside Bangkok's Bottoms Up club. He knew that a single gold-plated bullet would be enough to finish the job.

A single golden bullet did for Gibson. Before anyone could stop him, Scaramanga's manservant, Nick Nack,

I may be small but I'm never bullied!

Nick Nack

NICK NACK

The diminutive Nick Nack was Scaramanga's manservant and accomplice. He operated the controls of Scaramanga's Fun House. This was where the master assassin pitted his skills against invited guests who, with the notable exception of Bond, never came out alive. Nick Nack was also a *cordon bleu* chef and equally handy with a knife outside the kitchen.

Bond had killed Scaramanga and was sailing away with Mary Goodnight when Nick Nack, avenging his master, made a nuisance of himself.

THE SPY WHO LOVED ME™

The disappearance of a British and a Soviet nuclear submarine brings together James Bond of MI6 and Major Anya Amasova of the KGB in an unprecedented alliance. Recently stolen microfilm of a revolutionary submarine tracking system contains a clue that points to shipping magnate Karl Stromberg. Meanwhile, Stromberg has sent his top enforcer, Jaws, to eliminate anyone who comes in contact with his missing microfilm. Bond and Anya are soon fighting off Jaws, as well as other assassins. Bond, Anya and the US Navy finally close in on Stromberg's operation and discover the terrifying scope of his masterplan.

Observe, Mr. Bond, the instruments of Armageddon.

Karl Stromberg

With the capture of Bond and
Major Anya Amasova, Karl Stromberg
believed that the last obstacles to
his scheme had been overcome.

STROMBERG

He was a visionary – but a visionary with little love
for the human race. Captured by Stromberg's
supertanker *Liparus,* Bond, Anya and the crew of the
USS *Wayne* joined a British and Soviet nuclear sub
in the ship's hold. Stromberg triumphantly revealed
his plan: to use the subs' missiles to provoke world
war. With civilization in ruins, Stromberg would rule
the planet from his city beneath the sea.

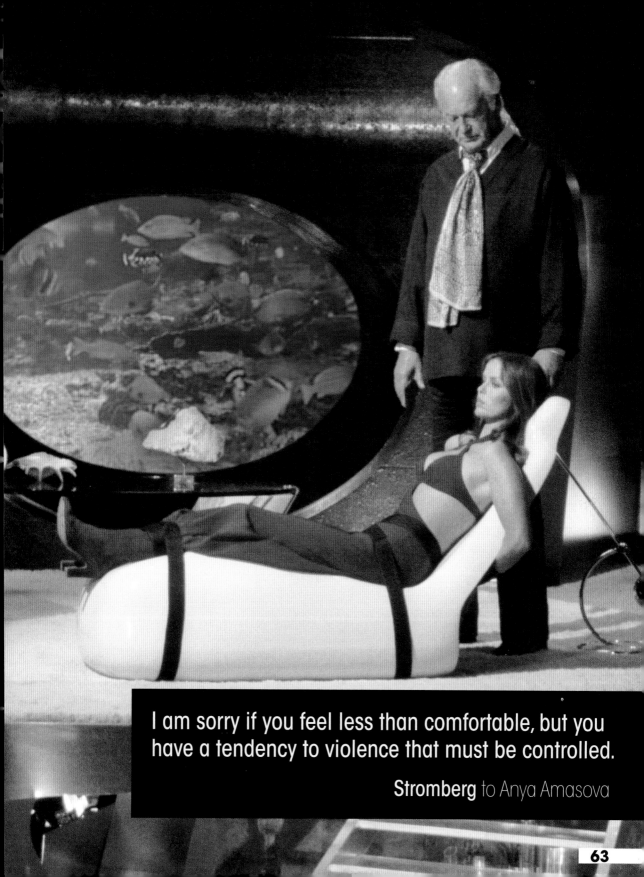

I am sorry if you feel less than comfortable, but you have a tendency to violence that must be controlled.

Stromberg to Anya Amasova

He just dropped in for a quick bite.

Bond to Anya Amasova

JAWS
of DEATH

Bond and Major Anya Amasova were on board the overnight train to Sardinia to investigate Karl Stromberg. Anya opened a cupboard – to reveal the towering, menacing figure of Jaws. It took all of Bond's quick wits to eject the steel-toothed man-mountain.

Bond attempted to give Jaws something else to chew on, apart from himself.

MOONRAKER™

A US space shuttle is hijacked while being transported by the RAF. Bond's investigations lead to Hugo Drax, whose aerospace empire designed the spacecraft. A chilly reception and a series of attacks on his life arouse Bond's suspicions. Drax is reportedly obsessed with the conquest of space. Bond, aided by the CIA's Dr. Holly Goodhead, discovers the scope of Drax's obsession. His ambitions are world-encompassing.

Look after Mr. Bond. See that some harm comes to him.

Hugo Drax to Chang

HUGO
DRAX

James Bond. You appear with the tedious inevitability of an unloved season.

Hugo Drax

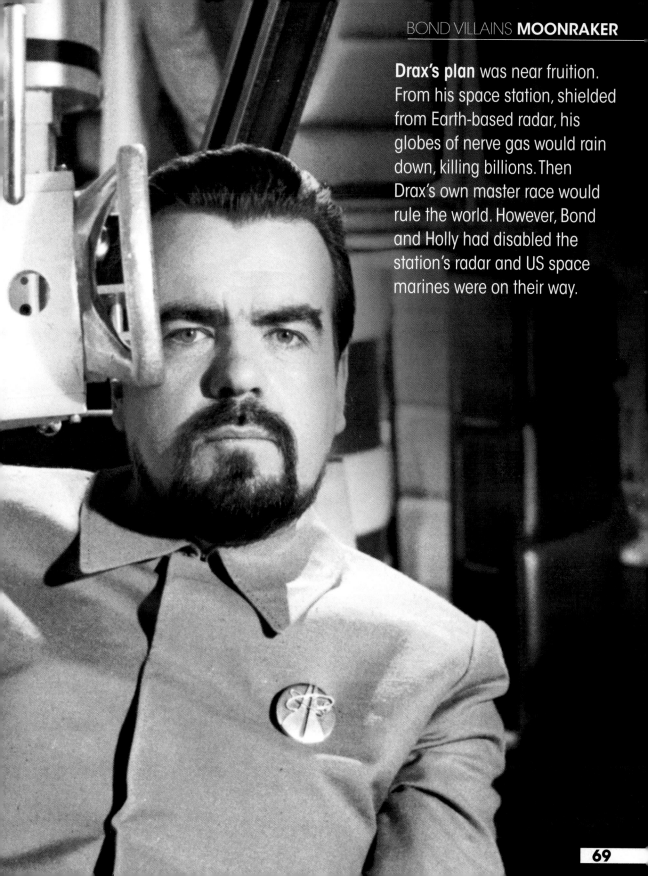

Drax's plan was near fruition. From his space station, shielded from Earth-based radar, his globes of nerve gas would rain down, killing billions. Then Drax's own master race would rule the world. However, Bond and Holly had disabled the station's radar and US space marines were on their way.

JAWS

Jaws brought Bond, dripping wet from a battle with Drax's pet anaconda, to Drax's rocket base in the South American jungle. Drax boasted of his plan to exterminate the world's population. He then told Jaws to secure Bond inside a room that lay beneath the jets of a shuttle set for take-off.

> Jaws, Mr. Bond must be cold after his swim. Place him where he can be assured of warmth.
>
> Hugo Drax

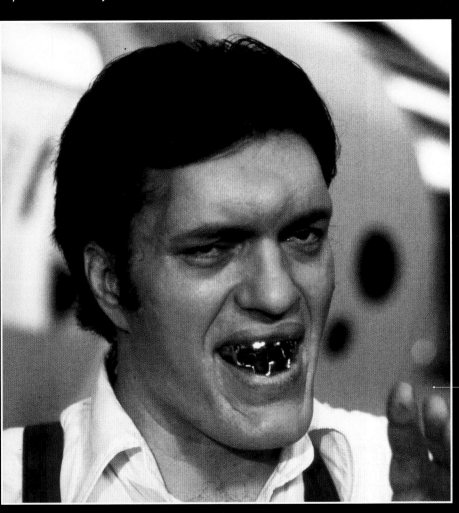

Jaws was happy to obey Drax's commands, until he realized that his face did not fit in Drax's plan for a master race of beautiful people to repopulate Earth.

FOR YOUR EYES ONLY

The sinking of the British spy ship *St. Georges* off the Albanian coast sparks a clandestine race to salvage a top-secret ATAC transmitter between MI6 and the KGB. Bond finds himself up against duplicitous shipping magnate Aris Kristatos, who poses as a friend to Britain, but plots to sell the transmitter to the KGB. Part of his plan is for Bond to locate the ATAC for him, then meet an untimely fate.

Bind that wound. We don't want
any blood in the water. Not yet.

KRISTATOS

MI6's Greek contact seemed keen to help Bond recover the ATAC, warning of the danger from underworld boss Milos Columbo. Kristatos was a smooth operator – but it would not be long before this shark in human form showed his teeth.

I must warn you, stopping Columbo will be difficult… You cannot just arrest him. You must find a different way. You may have to kill him.

Kristatos to Bond

EMILE LOCQUE

The man we want is Emile Leopold Locque… He's been convicted of several particularly brutal murders.

Bond

The distinctive spectacles favoured by Locque helped Bond and Q to identify this former enforcer from the Brussels underworld. Locque was involved in the assassination of MI6 agents the Havelocks and had murdered the charming Countess Lisl. Bond decided that the world would be better off without Locque running amok.

Warmongering General Orlov exploits the opportunities offered by a travelling circus to plant a nuclear bomb in a US air base in West Germany. The circus is owned by fabulously wealthy jewel smuggler Octopussy. She knows nothing of the plot – unlike her associates, Kamal Khan and his henchman Gobinda.

The West is decadent and divided.

Khan was disturbed to find
that Octopussy did not seem
overly concerned about Bond.
In fact, she seemed to like him.

KAMAL KHAN

Octopussy's smuggling operation had brought Kamal Khan wealth and power, but he wanted more. A deal with General Orlov to switch a consignment of smuggled Russian art treasures for a nuclear bomb seemed the perfect opportunity. Bond must not be allowed to spoil his plans.

> Mr. Bond is indeed a very rare breed. Soon to be made extinct.
>
> Kamal Khan

GOBINDA

Immensely strong, the looming, sinister Gobinda provided the muscle to back up Kamal Khan's wily manoeuvrings. This normally impassive enforcer developed a special hatred for Bond, leading him to go to almost any lengths to prevent Bond meddling in Kamal Khan's affairs.

> **The Englishman has escaped!**
> He won't go very far. We'll track him.
>
> **Gobinda** and Kamal Khan

A VIEW TO A KILL™

Microchip mogul Max Zorin is one of the strangest villains Bond has ever encountered. The product of Nazi steroid experiments, he possesses a genius-level IQ, but his intelligence has the merciless logic of the psychopath. Zorin wishes to control the world market in microchips; nothing short of the total destruction of California's Silicon Valley will satisfy him.

I'm sure I've seen him somewhere before.
Have security keep a good eye on him.

May Day and Zorin observe Bond

MAX ZORIN

Bond had destroyed Zorin's dream of ruling the world microchip market. California's Silicon Valley had not been destroyed by an earthquake. Bond had even thwarted Zorin's vengeance by tethering his airship to the Golden Gate Bridge. Zorin seized a fire axe to kill his arch foe. But Zorin's own doom was fast approaching.

Zorin and his partner May Day tried to ensure that Bond and geologist Stacey Sutton went to their deaths in a fire at San Francisco's City Hall.

MAY DAY

Zorin's lover, May Day, was almost as amoral and ruthless as he was. Abnormally strong, a martial arts expert, May Day was an assassin who really enjoyed her work. Yet, despite her heartless exterior, she retained a small spark of humanity, as Bond would discover.

Realizing that Zorin had no love for her, May Day sacrificed her life by riding Zorin's bomb out of his flooded mine and preventing a calamitous earthquake.

I see you're a woman
of very few words.

Bond to May Day

THE LIVING DAYLIGHTS™

The KGB's General Georgi Koskov defects to the West, claiming that the current KGB chief, General Pushkin, is masterminding a murder campaign against British agents. Before Koskov can explain further, he is kidnapped, ostensibly by the KGB. Bond is instructed to assassinate Pushkin, but doubts Koskov's story. Bond's investigations lead him into violent encounters with Koskov's co-conspirators: the assassin Necros and war-obsessed arms dealer Brad Whitaker.

I'm sorry, James. For you I have great affection, but we have an old saying: duty has no sweethearts.

We have an old saying, too, Georgi. And you're full of it.

General Georgi Koskov and Bond

> Murder will follow murder. Soviet and Western intelligence could destroy each other. God forbid, this could lead to nuclear war!
>
> General Georgi Koskov
> debriefs MI6

KOSKOV'S CONSPIRACY

It ranked as one of MI6's most humiliating episodes. The assassin Necros, disguised as a milkman, had burst into a safe house and spirited away KGB defector General Georgi Koskov. MI6 did not realize that the kidnap was part of Koskov's ingenious plan to kill the existing KGB chief, install himself in his place and make a fortune from an arms-for-drugs deal.

In Afghanistan, the supposedly kidnapped Koskov supervised a deal with the leader of opium traders the Snow Leopard Brotherhood.

Bond surprised the arms dealer while he was re-enacting the battle of Gettysburg with his soldiers.

BRAD
WHITAKER

Brad Whitaker was in love with war and idolized the famous – and notorious – military leaders of history: Caesar, Napoleon, Hitler. Following Bond's destruction of Whitaker and Koskov's plane-load of opium in Afghanistan, the CIA and Bond closed in on Whitaker's mansion in Tangier, where Koskov was also hiding out. Bond went in alone.

> Right. You've had your eight. Now I'll have my eighty!
>
> Brad Whitaker
> to Bond

LICENCE TO KILL™

South American drug baron Franz Sanchez is one of America's Most Wanted. He confirms his merciless reputation when he escapes police custody and mutilates Felix Leiter who, with Bond, helped capture him. Sanchez does not stop there: he orders the murder of Leiter's bride. However, Sanchez's hot-tempered cruelty also proves his weakness – a weakness Bond plays upon when he temporarily abandons MI6 and sets out to avenge Leiter. Bond infiltrates Sanchez's organization and tricks the gang boss into turning on his own associates. Bond then goes on the attack, finishing Sanchez for good.

I just want you to know that this is nothing personal. It's purely business.
Killing me won't stop anything, Sanchez!
There are worse things than dying, *hombre*.

Franz Sanchez and Felix Leiter

FRANZ SANCHEZ

The drug baron ruled by fear, making an example of anyone, whether friend or foe, who crossed him. Put under pressure first by Bond's cunning and then by his full-on attacks, Sanchez snapped, turning on the key members of his team until he alone remained.

It's a wise gambler who knows when his luck has run out.

Sanchez to Bond

Where's my wife?
Don't worry. We gave her
a nice honeymoooon!

Felix Leiter and Dario

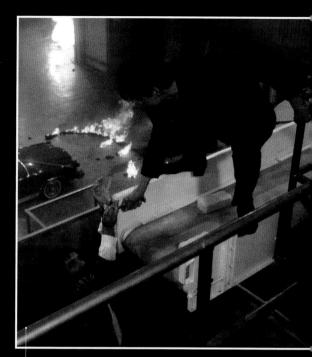

Bond clung desperately to the end of
a conveyor belt leading to a cocaine
pulverizer. Dario believed he had his
enemy at his mercy. He was wrong.

DARIO

He was Sanchez's favourite. The drug
lord could rely on Dario to execute his
orders, however merciless they were,
such as the murder of Felix Leiter's
bride. It was Dario who exposed Bond
as a spy at Sanchez's cocaine lab,
and Dario who gleefully sent Bond
seemingly to certain death.

GOLDENEYE™

A tense encounter with former Soviet fighter pilot Xenia Onatopp leads Bond to investigate the Janus crime syndicate, implicated in the theft of the top-secret GoldenEye weapons system. A reunion with Alec Trevelyan, a friend believed killed long ago on an MI6 mission, awaits Bond in St. Petersburg. Somehow, Bond must stop Trevelyan acting out his fantasies of revenge against Britain.

Back from the dead... no longer just an anonymous star on the memorial wall at MI6.

To the victor the spoils.

Alec Trevelyan

ALEC
TREVELYAN

Alec Trevelyan was enjoying being back from the dead. He had tricked MI6 into believing he had been killed in action and he was now about to return Britain, a country he loathed, to the Dark Ages with his stolen GoldenEye weapons system. To improve his mood even more, Natalya Simonova, sole witness to his organization's theft of the GoldenEye, was in his power. Trevelyan planned to enjoy his victory to the full. He had forgotten about Bond.

XENIA
ONATOPP

Bond was intrigued by the stunning Xenia Onatopp. She was a woman who enjoyed taking risks. Checking up on her, Bond found that she had links to the Janus crime syndicate. He would later discover just how important she was to Janus' masterplan and experience first-hand the violence that raged within her.

Onatopp's embraces were a little too physical for Bond's liking.

Nice to meet you, Mr. Bond.
The pleasure, I'm sure, was all mine.

Xenia Onatopp and Bond

Elliot Carver wields enormous power over much of the world. His news empire makes or breaks governments by influencing public opinion. Despite this, the rapacious media mogul is unsatisfied. One major market remains beyond his reach: China. Carver hatches a scheme to create a state of war between Britain and China and enable his own man to take over the Chinese government. In addition to exclusive media rights, Carver's news services will achieve a series of spectacular scoops, literally living up to the Carver Media Group's motto: Tomorrow's News Today!

Soon I'll have reached out and influenced more people than anybody in the history of the planet, save God himself.

Elliot Carver

ELLIOT CARVER

One of Carver's axioms was "There's no news like bad news". To gain more power for himself and his media group he was willing to create his own bad news, whatever the cost in human life. Nothing and no one, certainly not MI6 and James Bond, was going to stand in his way.

The distance between insanity and genius is measured only by success.

Elliot Carver

DOCTOR KAUFMAN

He was a master of undetectable murder and torture. As ordered by Elliot Carver, Dr. Kaufman had disposed of Paris, Carver's unfaithful wife, with his usual efficiency. Now just Bond remained. The Carver Media Group had already prepared news reports of the two deaths.

"**I'm just a professional** doing a job."
Kaufman's appeal fell on deaf ears.
He was about to pay for the murder of
Paris Carver, a woman Bond had loved.

The World Is Not Enough™

Renard is one of the world's most-feared terrorists. He is also dying from a bullet in his brain. But before that happy day for the rest of humanity, Renard plans to destroy the city of Istanbul, so that the pipeline owned by the woman he adores can monopolize oil distribution to the West. She was once his kidnap victim. Her name is Elektra King and she has a score to settle with her father, M and MI6.

I usually hate killing an unarmed man.
Cold-blooded murder is a filthy business...
But in your case I feel nothing. Just like you.

Bond to Renard

ELEKTRA KING

She liked to think that no one, especially men, could resist her. But Bond, her soon-to-be late lover, retained allegiance to M, whom Elektra hated. She blamed M – and Bond – for using her as bait to catch Renard. Now she would have the pleasure of Bond's slow death in her torture chair.

> I could have given you the world. **The world is not enough.** Foolish sentiment. **Family motto.**
>
> Elektra and **Bond**

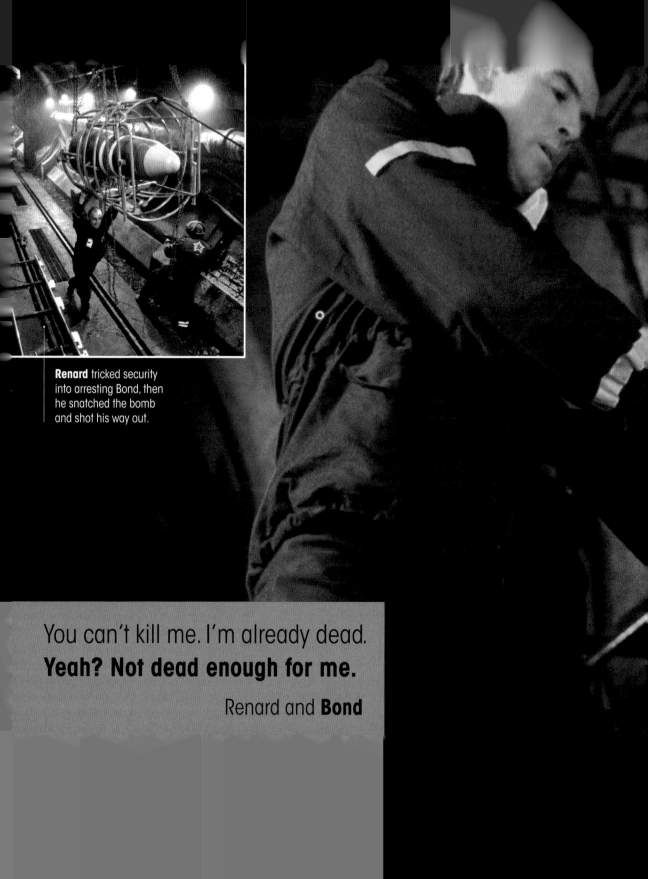

Renard tricked security into arresting Bond, then he snatched the bomb and shot his way out.

You can't kill me. I'm already dead.
Yeah? Not dead enough for me.

Renard and **Bond**

RENARD

Bond believed that he had foiled Renard's attempt to steal a nuclear weapon from a former Soviet test site. But Renard was undaunted. The bullet in his brain had robbed him of the ability to feel pain. He also knew Bond's weak spot: his feelings for the beautiful Elektra King. Renard exploited this knowledge to buy himself valuable time.

DIE ANOTHER DAY

No one knows much about Gustav Graves. The diamond magnate seems to have risen without trace, his success capturing the British public's imagination, as well as earning him a knighthood. Graves is a self-proclaimed visionary. With his enormous wealth he has created the Icarus space mirror, a miraculous device he claims will make deserts bloom. Bond discovers that Graves (in reality corrupt North Korean army officer Colonel Moon, radically altered by gene therapy) dreams of using Icarus, not for peaceful purposes, but to destroy South Korea and create a new superpower.

I have to live my dreams.

Gustav Graves

GUSTAV GRAVES

He believed he had the whole world fooled. Gustav Graves had used gene therapy to alter his appearance and change his identity. He was no longer Colonel Moon of the North Korean Army, but a world-famous diamond magnate. Graves also had an ace in the hole – his double agent lover, Miranda Frost of MI6.

On board his flying HQ, Graves donned a battlesuit that doubled as the controls for Icarus and unleashed the weapon's might on South Korea's defences.

You see, Mr. Bond, you can't kill my dreams. But my dreams can kill you.

Gustav Graves

An informer inside MI6 enabled Zao to alert Colonel Moon: James Bond had infiltrated their operation.

ZAO

The North Korean terrorist had a lucrative racket with NK army officer Colonel Moon trading arms for African conflict diamonds. Then Bond intervened and a case of diamonds exploded in Zao's face. Bond was captured and Zao sought a new identity, but not even gene therapy could hide him from Bond.

CASINO ROYALE

MI6 only know him as Le Chiffre, "The Cipher". He is a maths genius and an expert poker player, his only weakness a tendency to weep blood under pressure. Le Chiffre is also a banker to terrorists and has been speculating with his clients' ill-gotten gains by using terrorist tactics to manipulate stock values. Bond, MI6's newest double-O agent, prevents one of his operatives from blowing up an airliner and Le Chiffre loses over $100 million. To save his skin, he organizes a poker game for high rollers at Montenegro's Casino Royale. Le Chiffre has to win. M sends Bond to make sure he doesn't.

You've changed your shirt, Mr. Bond. I do hope our little game isn't causing you to perspire?

A little. But I won't consider myself to be in trouble until I start weeping blood.

Le Chiffre and **Bond**

LE CHIFFRE

Weeping blood comes merely from a derangement of the tear duct – nothing sinister.

Le Chiffre

Defeated by Bond at poker, Le Chiffre was not finished yet. He kidnapped Bond's colleague, Vesper Lynd, and caused Bond to crash his Aston Martin by throwing her out onto the road. One of Le Chiffre's men cut a tracking device from Bond's arm and the infuriating spy was in Le Chiffre's power at last. All Le Chiffre needed was the bank account password. The winnings – $115 million – would be his, and his life would be safe.

> Money isn't as valuable to our organization as knowing who to trust.
>
> **Mr. White** to Le Chiffre

MR. WHITE

His organization, Quantum, had given
Le Chiffre every chance to recoup his
losses, but Le Chiffre had proved inefficient
as well as untrustworthy. The money could
wait – Vesper Lynd could attend to that.
More importantly, Quantum's worldwide
reputation was at stake. Le Chiffre must die.

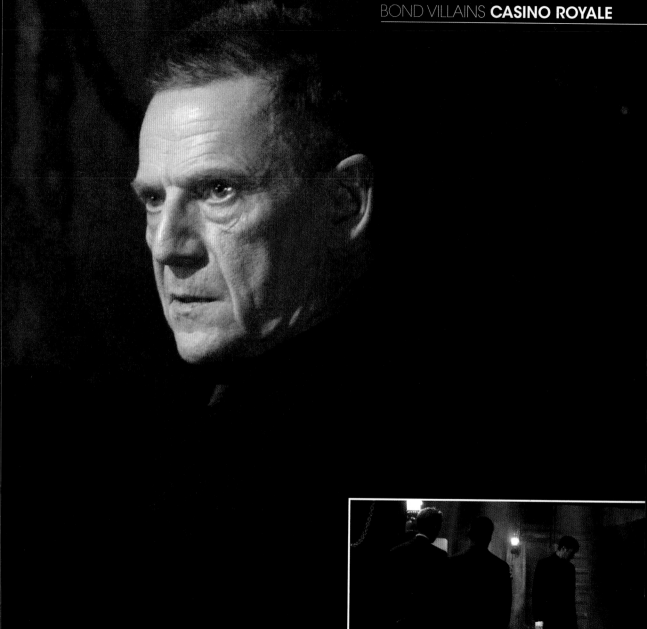

GETTLER

In his panama hat and spectacles with one dark lens, the man was at once noticeable and slightly sinister. Vesper Lynd knew him immediately: Gettler of Quantum. She also knew that her brief happiness with Bond was over. Now she had to betray the man she had grown to love. The meeting was arranged. The money withdrawn from the bank. But Bond had followed her.

Bond had been willing to quit MI6 out of love for Vesper. These dreams came crashing down as he witnessed her betrayal. He wanted vengeance.

QUANTUM OF SOLACE

Dominic Greene is CEO of worldwide utilities company Greene Planet. He is also a prominent member of Quantum, a secret organization of immense power whose tentacular reach embraces corruption, terrorism and the manipulation of governments. Greene spearheads Quantum's latest plan: the control of Bolivia's water supply in exchange for masterminding a coup by exiled dictator General Medrano. Greene enlists the support of the CIA and the British government with phoney promises of oil rights. He is confident the CIA will assist him by removing a minor problem: a rogue British agent named James Bond.

We've already begun destabilizing the government. We'll supply the security. We'll pay off the right officials. And we have 26 countries ready to officially recognize your new Bolivian government.

Dominic Greene of Quantum
to General Medrano

DOMINIC GREENE

Greene knew Camille did not love him. He was convinced she was a spy, meddling with his plans to install General Medrano as Bolivian president and gain control of the country's water. Greene wanted rid of her. He decided to give her to Medrano, as a plaything.

Camille protested her innocence, but Greene was not fooled. His suave manner concealed a vicious streak. He did not forgive or forget.

There is nothing that makes me more uncomfortable than friends talking behind my back. Feels like... ants under my skin.

Dominic Greene to Camille

I knew your family. Sadly, I believe
I was the last to see them alive.

General Medrano to Camille

GENERAL MEDRANO

He was brutal and sadistic, but Medrano was no fool. He knew that "getting into bed" with Quantum was risky. But how else was he to regain power? Any concerns he had were forgotten when he laid eyes on the girl proffered by Dominic Greene to "sweeten the deal": Camille Montes, the beautiful daughter of an old, dead, enemy.

MUTUAL HATRED

Medrano saw the loathing in Camille's eyes. The sight spurred him on. She had burst into his room, threatened him with a gun and robbed him of his fun with a hotel receptionist. She would pay with her life. Eventually. He had her cornered, but Camille was quick, too quick…

Now your face has the same
look of fear as your mother's did.

General Medrano *to Camille*

James Bond will return...

Senior Editor Alastair Dougall
Designer Owen Bennett
Managing Editor Catherine Saunders
Art Director Lisa Lanzarini
Publishing Manager Simon Beecroft
Category Publisher Alex Allan
Production Editor Clare McLean
Production Controller Nick Seston

First published in Great Britain in 2010
by Dorling Kindersley Limited, 80 Strand, London, WC2R 0RL

10 11 12 13 14   10 9 8 7 6 5 4 3 2 1
177927 – 07/10

007 [Gun Logo] and related James Bond Trademarks
© 1962-2010 Danjaq, LLC and United Artists Corporation.
All rights reserved. 007 [Gun Logo] and related James Bond Trademarks
are trademarks of Danjaq, LLC, licensed by EON Productions Limited.

Page design copyright © 2010 Dorling Kindersley Limited

All rights reserved. No part of this publication may be reproduced,
stored in a retrieval system, or transmitted in any form or by any means,
electronic, mechanical, photocopying, recording, or otherwise, without
the prior written permission of the copyright owner.

A CIP catalogue record for this book is available from the British Library

ISBN: 978-1-4053-5537-7

Scanning and retouching by MDP, UK
Colour proofing by Alta Image, UK
Printed and bound in China by Leo Paper Products Ltd

Discover more at www.dk.com

The author and Dorling Kindersley would like to thank Jenni McMurrie
of EON Productions for her invaluable help during the production of this book.